Crea

The Wisdom of Hildegard of Bingen

Translated by Mother Columba Hart and Jane Bishop
Edited and with an introduction by
Kathleen A. Walsh

PAULIST PRESS
New York ◆ Mahwah, N.J.

Cover design by Tim McKeen. Cover photo by Don Kimball.

Library of Congress Cataloging-in-Publication Data

Hildegard, Saint, 1098-1179
    [Scivias. English. Selections]
    Creation and Christ : the wisdom of Hildegard of Bingen / translated by
Columba Hart and Jane Bishop ; edited and with an introduction by
Kathleen A. Walsh.
        p.   cm.
    Includes bibliographical references (p.   ).
    ISBN 0-8091-3674-0 (alk. paper)
    1. Mysticism—Catholic Church—Early works to 1800. 2. Catholic
Church—Doctrines—Early works to 1800. I. Hart, Columba, 1903-. II.
Bishop, Jane, 1950- . III. Walsh, Kathleen A. IV. Title.
BV5080.H54213 1996   96–12796
248.2′2–dc20   CIP

Published by Paulist Press
997 Macarthur Boulevard
Mahwah, New Jersey 07430

Printed and bound in the
United States of America

CONTENTS

Introduction   1

The *Scivias*

Declaration:
These are true visions flowing from God   11

Book One: The Creator and Creation   16
1. God Enthroned Shows Himself to Hildegard   16
2. Creation and the Fall (excerpts)   21

Book Two: The Redeemer and Redemption   41
1. The Redeemer   41

Book Three: The History of Salvation
Symbolized by a Building   59
1. God and Man   59

Suggestions for Further Reading   88

INTRODUCTION

*S*t. Hildegard of Bingen (1098–1179) was a fascinating woman whose achievements reveal both her keen intellectual abilities and her forceful personality. She founded and led the Benedictine community at Bingen and worked tirelessly as an author, preacher and reformer. Indeed, Hildegard was a prolific writer, and the depth of her insights was matched by the breadth of her interests. Her writings not only dealt with issues of theology and spirituality but also explored the areas of music, drama, medicine, and natural science. In terms of the body of her work, Hildegard would in any age be acknowledged as the accomplished writer and thinker that she was, but given the fact that she achieved such things during an age when few women dared to write, let alone do so in the name of God, shows her work to be truly courageous.

HILDEGARD'S LIFE

The last of ten children born to a noble family in Bermersheim, Germany, Hildegard was dedicated to the service of God by her parents, Hildebert and Mechthild, in 1106. Just eight years old at the time, Hildegard was placed in the care of a noblewoman named Jutta, daughter of the Count of Sponheim, who lived as a recluse in a cottage adjoining the church of the abbey founded by St. Disibod. Although of a rather sickly constitution, she served as Jutta's handmaid and servant, in return receiving instruction in Latin, religion and an array of domestic skills. Hildegard herself professed her virginity formally as a teenager, by which time other women had joined her and Jutta, and the hermitage had become a convent of the Benedictine rule.

After her entrance into the hermitage little is known of Hildegard's life there until Jutta's death in 1136, at which time Hildegard succeeded her as abbess of the community. Yet Hildegard's own reflections on these early years reveal a mysterious and active interior life, marked by unusual experiences, visions and an ability to foretell the future. The visions were characterized by a strange brightness and yielded up various shapes and figures, which she interpreted with the help of a heavenly voice. Initially they confused and frightened Hildegard, provoking fits of crying and fleeting thoughts of suicide, and it was only after many years and much reflection that she came to understand them as vehicles of divine revelation. She told no one of them at first except Jutta, but after her accession to abbess she felt increasingly compelled to write the visions down. She finally entrusted knowledge of the visions to her confessor, the monk Godfrey, who, with Hildegard's acquiescence, related the matter to his abbot, Conon. The abbot asked her to write down some of the revelations that God had shown her, and when she did so, they were submitted to the Archbishop of Mainz, who authenticated the claim that they were from God. Subsequently, the monk Volmar was appointed by the abbot to serve as her secretary.

Almost immediately afterward, Hildegard began the dictation of the *Scivias*. Short for *Scito vias Domini or Know the Ways of the Lord*, this collection of twenty-six visions took her ten years to complete. Her call to write the *Scivias*, received in 1141 and related in her *Declaration* about the work, consisted of "a fiery light of exceeding brilliance" that endowed her with a sure knowledge of the meaning of the scriptures. She was commanded to "speak these things that you see and hear. And write them not by yourself or any other human being, but by the will of Him Who knows, sees and disposes all things in the secrets of His mysteries."

Although she had been doubtful at first about her role as visionary and prophet, she had come to embrace her charism. Her confidence was further bolstered by the positive reaction the unfinished manuscript of the *Scivias* received from Pope Eugenius III. Having been presented with the work by the Archbishop of Mainz during the winter of 1147–1148, Pope Eugenius set up a commission to examine Hildegard's visionary writings. After receiving a favorable report, the pope not only read and discussed the work with his advisors, he authorized Hildegard to publish it.

This official approval helped Hildegard in wrestling with her own doubts about the nature of her prophetic mission, and indeed in many ways her work stands in the tradition of the prophetic works of the Old Testament.* The prophet is one who calls the community back to fidelity and the moral life. In the mid-twelfth century, Hildegard saw a clergy who lacked dedication, sacred scriptures that were neglected and a Christian community left without proper instruction in

*For a further discussion of the prophetic characteristics of Hildegard's work see Barbara J. Newman's Introduction to *Hildegard of Bingen: Scivias* (Classics of Western Spirituality, Paulist Press, 1994).

4

the faith. Like the Hebrew prophets whose job it was to call the chosen people back to the covenant, Hildegard calls the community of faith back to its roots, speaking especially to the theologians, monks and priests who, "though they see the inmost contents of the Scriptures, do not wish to tell them or preach them, because they are lukewarm and sluggish in serving God's justice."

As she mentions in the *Scivias*, her call to the prophetic vocation came not because of her own fitness for the task or any exceptional holiness on her part. Like other prophets before her, Hildegard is humbled by God's choice of her, but education, gender, social status and eloquence neither confer nor remove the prophetic power that comes from God alone. Despite biblical and social restrictions regarding women's silence and submission, Hildegard felt herself called by God and was unable to do other than follow God's instruction. Her protestations of lowliness, lack of education and poor health that appear in the *Scivias* are literary conventions written to convince readers that it is through God's power alone that these visions and writings were accomplished, and her insistence on characterizing herself as simple was meant not as a literal truth but as a telling comment on the well-schooled clerics who needed her to "unlock for them the enclosure of mysteries that they, timid as they are, conceal in a hidden and fruitless field."

The *Scivias*, in its entirety, comprises three distinct sections that deal, in order, with creation, redemption and sanctification. Each of the three books consists of a number of visions that work on the levels of allegory, prophecy and theology. The visions themselves contain a brief description of what Hildegard saw and a commentary on the vision, often highlighted by scriptural texts. Together these visions and commentaries give us a comprehensive view of God's relationship to his people, the sacrifice of Christ and the securing of human salvation, and the leif of the Church, including such things as sacramental practice and marriage issues. With its visions, doctrinal discussions, allegorical stories, apocalyptic prophecies and dense symbolism, the work is one of great depth and complexity.

The *Scivias* remained the most well known of Hildegard's works during her lifetime. Its popularity was due in part to the official ecclesiastical approval it received, but also in part to the beautiful illuminations that appeared in the early manuscript (which some attribute to Hildegard herself). Yet it constitutes but a fraction of her voluminous literary output. During the decade following 1150, the period which saw Hildegard move her community to Rupertsberg in Bingen, Hildegard composed instructional materials dealing with theology and doctrine as well as liturgical hymns and music, a morality play called the *Ordo Virtutum*, and fifty allegorical homilies for use in the newly formed community of sisters. In addition, her sizable correspondence attests to the many outside contacts that Hildegard cultivated during these years, including both ecclesiastical leaders and an impressive array of secular rulers and lay persons.

Her great interest in natural science and medicine is revealed in several works on these subjects, including *The Book of Simple Medicine* and *Causes and Cures*. Finally, Hildegard also composed two other major visionary works, *Liber vitae meritorum (Book of Life's Merits),* based on her experience as a spiritual director, and *Liber divinorum operum (Book of Divine Works),* which delves into history and eschatology. Her writings, combined with lengthy preaching tours throughout Germany, kept her busy in her later years. Despite increasing frailty and frequent illness, Hildegard continued right up until her death on

September 17, 1179, to pursue the activities of counseling, preaching, writing and instructing that constituted her life's work.

The selections from the *Scivias* here presented include visions from each book. From Book One, entitled *The Creator and Creation*, visions one and two are presented. The first, *God Enthroned Shows Himself to Hildegard*, reflects on the greatness and majesty of God, showing in relief the humility of humanity and extolling the virtues of fear of the Lord and poverty of spirit. The second vision, *Creation and the Fall* (here presented in excerpted form), details the fall of Lucifer and his angels, the creation of hell and the fall of the human race. Adam and Eve's ejection from paradise and the introduction of disharmony into the world are explored in light of the salvation brought by the Son.

The Redeemer, the initial vision from Book Two, *The Redeemer and Redemption*, summarizes many of the themes of the first book, including the fall of Adam and Eve. The main focus, however, is on the role and person of Christ as the Word of the Father. The overcoming of the darkness and sin of the world is described as the gradual introduction of the light of God's salvation

8

beginning with the patriarchs, then the prophets, John the Baptist, and finally and fully in Christ.

In the third book, *The History of Salvation Symbolized by a Building*, the first vision entitled *God and Man* confirms Hildegard's call and explores the nature of humanity as created and as saved. Despite the weaknesses and failings of humanity, God holds us to himself. Hildegard speaks of the paradox of human beings who are but "poor, weak, infirm mire" and yet are exalted by the fact that "the Son of the Most High God has human form in Himself."

As the reader will see, the *Scivias* is marked by a theological sophistication and a religious symbolism beautiful in its complexity and startling in its imagery. Hildegard's wisdom in matters of the spiritual life and religion is well demonstrated in this work, where she shows a unique ability to communicate the realities of the sinful human condition and the depth of God's abiding love for his people. Although these excerpts of her work cannot possibly represent the depth and breadth of her many theological and prophetic insights, they provide the reader with a starting point for exploring with this magnificent thinker the mysteries at the heart of the Christian life.

DECLARATION

THESE ARE TRUE VISIONS FLOWING FROM GOD

*A*nd behold! In the forty-third year of my earthly course, as I was gazing with great fear and trembling attention at a heavenly vision, I saw a great splendor in which resounded a voice from Heaven, saying to me,

"O fragile human, ashes of ashes, and filth of filth! Say and write what you see and hear. But since you are timid in speaking, and simple in expounding, and untaught in writing, speak and write these things not by a human mouth, and not by the understanding of human invention, and not by the requirements of human composition, but as you see and hear them on high in the heavenly places in the wonders of God. Explain these things in such a way that the hearer, receiving the words of his instructor, may expound them in those words, according to that will, vision and instruction. Thus therefore, O human, speak these things that you see and hear. And write them not by yourself or any other human being, but by the will of

Him Who knows, sees and disposes all things in the secrets of His mysteries."

And again I heard the voice from Heaven saying to me, "Speak therefore of these wonders, and, being so taught, write them and speak."

It happened that, in the eleven hundred and forty-first year of the Incarnation of the Son of God, Jesus Christ, when I was forty-two years and seven months old, Heaven was opened and a fiery light of exceeding brilliance came and permeated my whole brain and inflamed my whole heart and my whole breast, not like a burning but like a warming flame, as the sun warms anything its rays touch. And immediately I knew the meaning of the exposition of the Scriptures, namely the Psalter, the Gospel and the other Catholic volumes of both the Old and the New Testaments, though I did not have the interpretation of the words of their texts or the division of the syllables or the knowledge of cases or tenses. But I had sensed in myself wonderfully the power and mystery of secret and admirable visions from my childhood—that is, from the age of five—up to that time, as I do now. This, however, I showed to no one except a few religious persons who were living in the same manner as I; but meanwhile, until the time when God by His grace wished it to be manifested, I concealed it in quiet silence. But the visions I saw I did not perceive in dreams, or sleep, or delirium, or by the eyes of the body, or by the ears of the outer self, or in hidden places; but I received them while awake and seeing with a pure mind and the eyes and ears of the inner self, in open places, as God willed it. How this might be is hard for mortal flesh to understand.

But when I had passed out of childhood and had reached the age of full maturity mentioned above, I heard a voice from Heaven saying, "I am the Living Light, Who illuminates the darkness. The person [Hildegard] whom I have chosen and whom I have miraculously stricken as I willed, I have placed among great wonders, beyond the measure of the ancient people who saw in Me many secrets; but I have laid her low on the earth, that she might not set herself up in arrogance of mind. The world has had in her no joy or lewdness or use in worldly things, for I have withdrawn her from impudent boldness, and she feels fear and is timid in her works. For she suffers in her inmost being and in the veins of her flesh; she is distressed in mind and sense and endures great pain of body

13

because no security has dwelt in her, but in all her undertakings she has judged herself guilty. For I have closed up the cracks in her heart that her mind may not exalt itself in pride or vainglory, but may feel fear and grief rather than joy and wantonness. Hence in My love she searched in her mind as to where she could find someone who would run in the path of salvation. And she found such a one and loved him [the monk Volmar of Disibodenberg], knowing that he was a faithful man, working like herself on another part of the work that leads to Me. And holding fast to him, she worked with him in great zeal so that My hidden miracles might be revealed. And she did not seek to exalt herself above herself but with many sighs bowed to him whom she found in the ascent of humility and the intention of good will.

"O human, who receives these things meant to manifest what is hidden not in the disquiet of deception but in the purity of simplicity, write, therefore, the things you see and hear."

But I, though I saw and heard these things, refused to write for a long time through doubt and bad opinion and the diversity of human words, not with stubbornness but in the exercise of humility, until, laid low by the scourge of God, I fell upon a bed of sickness; then, compelled at last by many illnesses, and by the witness of a certain noble maiden of good conduct [the nun Richardis of Stade] and of that man whom I had secretly sought and found, as mentioned above, I set my hand to the writing. While I was doing it, I sensed, as I mentioned before, the deep profundity of scriptural exposition; and, raising myself from illness by the strength I received, I brought this work to a close—though just barely—in ten years.

These visions took place and these words were written in the days of Henry, Archbishop of Mainz, and of Conrad, King of the Romans, and of Cuno, Abbot of Disibodenberg, under Pope Eugenius.

And I spoke and wrote these things not by the invention of my heart or that of any other person, but as by the secret mysteries of God I heard and received them in the heavenly places.

And again I heard a voice from Heaven saying to me, "Cry out therefore, and write thus!"

FROM BOOK ONE:
THE CREATOR AND CREATION
VISION ONE
God Enthroned Shows Himself to Hildegard

I saw a great mountain the color of iron, and enthroned on it One of such great glory that it blinded my sight. On each side of him there extended a soft shadow, like a wing of wondrous breadth and length. Before him, at the foot of the mountain, stood an image full of eyes on all sides, in which, because of those eyes, I could discern no human form. In front of this image stood another, a child wearing a tunic of subdued color but white shoes, upon whose head such glory descended from the One enthroned upon that mountain that I could not look at its face. But from the One who sat enthroned upon that mountain many living sparks sprang forth, which flew very sweetly around the images. Also, I perceived in this mountain many little windows, in which appeared human heads, some of subdued colors and some white.

And behold, He Who was enthroned upon that mountain cried out in a strong, loud voice saying, "O human, who are fragile dust of the earth and ashes of ashes! Cry out and speak of the origin of pure salvation until those people are instructed, who, though they see the inmost contents of the Scriptures, do not wish to tell them or preach them, because they are lukewarm and sluggish in serving God's justice. Unlock for them the enclosure of mysteries that they, timid as they are, conceal in a hidden and fruitless field. Burst forth into a fountain of abundance and overflow with mystical knowledge, until they who now think you contemptible because of Eve's transgression are stirred up by the flood of your irrigation. For you have received your profound insight not from humans, but from the lofty and tremendous Judge on high, where this calmness will shine strongly with glorious light among the shining ones.

"Arise therefore, cry out and tell what is shown to you by the strong power of God's help, for He Who rules every creature in might and kindness floods those who fear Him and serve Him in sweet love and humility with the glory of heavenly enlightenment and leads those who persevere in the way of justice to the joys of the Eternal Vision."

1 The strength and stability of God's eternal Kingdom

As you see, therefore, *the great mountain the color of iron*, symbolizes the strength and stability of the eternal Kingdom of God, which no fluctuation of mutability can destroy; and the *One enthroned upon it of such great glory that it blinds your sight* is the One in the kingdom of beatitude Who rules the whole world with celestial divinity in the brilliance of unfading serenity, but is incomprehensible to human minds. But that *on each side of him there extends a soft shadow like a wing of wonderful breadth and length* shows that both in admonition and in punishment ineffable justice displays sweet and gentle protection and perseveres in true equity.

2 *Concerning fear of the Lord*

And before him at the foot of the mountain stands an image full of eyes on all sides. For the Fear of the Lord stands in God's presence with humility and gazes on the Kingdom of God, surrounded by the clarity of a good and just intention, exercising her zeal and stability among humans. And thus *you can discern no human form in her on account of those eyes.* For by the acute sight of her contemplation she counters all forgetfulness of God's justice, which people often feel in their mental tedium, so no inquiry by weak mortals eludes her vigilance.

3 Concerning those who are poor in spirit

And so *before this image appears another image, that of a child, wearing a tunic of subdued color but white shoes.* For when the Fear of the Lord leads, they who are poor in spirit follow; for the Fear of the Lord holds fast in humble devotion to the blessedness of poverty of spirit, which does not seek boasting or elation of heart, but loves simplicity and sobriety of mind, attributing its just works not to itself but to God in pale subjection, wearing, as it were, a tunic of subdued color and faithfully following the serene footsteps of the Son of God. *Upon her head descends such glory from the One enthroned upon that mountain that you cannot look at her face;* because He Who rules every created being imparts the power and strength of this blessedness by the great clarity of His visitation, and weak, mortal thought cannot grasp His purpose, since He Who possesses celestial riches submitted himself humbly to poverty.

4 They who fear God and love poverty of spirit are the guardians of virtues

But *from the One Who is enthroned upon that mountain many living sparks go forth, which fly about those images with great sweetness.* This means that many exceedingly strong virtues come forth from Almighty God, darting fire in divine glory; these ardently embrace and captivate those who truly fear God and who faithfully love poverty of spirit, surrounding them with their help and protection.

5 The aims of human acts cannot be hidden from God's knowledge

Wherefore *in this mountain you see many little windows, in which appear human heads, some of subdued color and some white.* For in the most high and profound and perspicuous knowledge of God the aims of human acts cannot be concealed or hidden. Most often they display both lukewarmness and purity, since people now slumber in guilt, weary in their hearts and in their deeds, and now awaken and keep watch in honor. Solomon bears witness to this for Me, saying:

6 Solomon on this subject

"The slothful hand has brought about poverty, but the hand of the industrious man prepares riches" [Prv 10:4]; which means, a person makes himself weak and poor when he will not work justice, or avoid wickedness, or pay a debt, remaining idle in the face of the wonders of the works of beatitude. But one who does strong works of salvation, running in the way of truth, obtains the upwelling fountain of glory, by which he prepares himself most precious riches on earth and in Heaven.

Therefore, whoever has knowledge in the Holy Spirit and wings of faith, let this one not ignore My admonition but taste it, embrace it and receive it in his soul.

VISION TWO
Creation and the Fall

Then I saw as it were a great multitude of very bright living lamps, which received fiery brilliance and acquired an unclouded splendor. And behold! A pit of great breadth and depth appeared, with a mouth like the mouth of a well, emitting fiery smoke with great stench, from which a loathsome cloud spread out and touched a deceitful, vein-shaped form. And, in a region of brightness, it blew upon a white cloud that had come forth from a beautiful human form and contained within itself many and many stars, and so doing, cast out both the white cloud and the human form from that region. When this was done, a luminous splendor surrounded that region, and all the elements of the world, which

21

before had existed in great calm, were turned to the greatest agitation and displayed horrible terrors. And again I heard Him Who had spoken to me before, saying:

1 No unjust impulse takes the blessed angels from the love and praise of God

No impulse of injustice makes those withdraw in terror who follow God with faithful devotion and burn with worthy love through affection for Him, from the glory of heavenly beatitude; while they who serve God merely in pretence not only fail to advance to greater things but, by just judgment, are cast out from the things they erroneously suppose they possess. This is shown by the *great multitude of very bright living lamps*; they are the vast army of heavenly spirits, shining in the blessed life and living in great beauty and adornment, because when they were created by God they did not grasp at proud exaltation but strongly persisted in divine love. For, *receiving fiery brilliance, they acquired an unclouded splendor*, because when Lucifer and his followers attempted to rebel against the supreme Creator, they, with zeal for God in his and his followers' downfall, clothed themselves in the vigilance of divine love, while the others, not wishing to know God, embraced

22

the torpor of ignorance. In what way? At the fall of the Devil great praise burst forth from these angelic spirits who persevered in rectitude with God, because with keenest sight they knew that God continues immovable, without any change of any mutability in His power, so that no warrior can ever conquer Him. And thus, burning in His love and persevering in righteousness, they despised all the dust of injustice.

2 Lucifer, for pride in his beauty and power, was cast forth from Heaven

But Lucifer, who because of his pride was cast forth from celestial glory, was so great at the moment of his creation that he felt no defect either in his beauty or in his strength. Hence when he contemplated his beauty, and when he considered in himself the power of his strength, he discovered pride, which promised him that he might begin what he wished, because he could achieve what he had begun. And, seeing a place where he thought he could live, wanting to display his beauty and power there, he spoke thus within himself about God: "I wish to shine there as He does here!" And all his army assented, saying, "What you wish we also wish." And when, elated with pride, he tried to achieve what he had conceived, the jealousy of the Lord, reaching out in fiery blackness, cast him down with all his retinue, so that they were made burning instead of shining and black instead of fair. Why did this happen?

3 God would have been unjust if He had not cast them down

If God had not cast down their presumption, He would have been unjust, since He would have cherished those who wished to divide the wholeness of divinity. But He cast them down and reduced their impiety to nothing, as He removes from the sight of His glory all who try to oppose themselves to Him, as My servant Job shows when he says:

4 Words of Job on this subject

"The lamp of the wicked shall be put out and a deluge shall come upon them; and He shall distribute the sorrows of His wrath. They shall be chaff before the face of the wind, and sparks scattered by the whirlwind" [Jb 21:17–18]. This means the flagrant filth of wanton wickedness that emerges from false prosperity, like a distinguishing mark on the carnal will of those who do not fear God but spurn Him in perverse rage, disdaining to know that anyone can conquer them, while in the fire of their ferocity they want to consume whatever they oppose. In the hour of God's vengeance this filth will be trodden underfoot like dirt; and by the supreme judgment these impious ones will be cast down in wrath by all who are under heaven, because they are harmful both to God and to humans. Therefore, since God does not allow them to have what they want, they are scattered everywhere among people, tormented by pain in the rage of their madness, because they burn to possess what God does not allow them to devour. And since they withdraw in this way from God, they become entirely useless, able to do nothing good for either God or humanity, cut off from the seed of life by the foreseeing eye of God's contemplation. For which reason they are given over to misery, wasting themselves in the flat taste of evil fame, since they do not receive the downpouring rain of the Holy Spirit.

5 On Hell, which in its voracity keeps souls swallowed up

But the *pit of great breadth and depth* that appeared to you is Hell, having within it, as you see, the breadth of vices and the depth of losses. It has a mouth indeed like the mouth of a well, emitting a fiery smoke with great stench, because in its voracity to swallow up souls, it shows them sweetness and gentleness, and with perverse deception leads them to the torments of perdition, where rises a burning fire with black smoke pouring out and a boiling, deadly stench; these dire torments were prepared for the Devil and his followers, who turned away from the Supreme Good, not wishing to know or understand it. Therefore they are outcast from all good, not because they did not know it, but because in their great pride they despised it. What does this mean?

6 In the casting down of the Devil Hell was created

In the casting down of the Devil this exterior darkness, full of all kinds of pains, was created; for these evil spirits, in contrast to the glory that had been prepared for them, were subject to the misery of many punishments, and in contrast to the brightness they had had, endured the thickest darkness. How? When the proud angel raised himself on high like a snake, he received the prison of Hell, because it could not be that anyone should prevail over God. For how could two hearts possibly exist in one breast? Likewise, there could not be two gods in Heaven. But since the Devil and his followers chose proud presumption, therefore he found the pit of Hell prepared for him. So also the people who imitate them in their actions become sharers of their pains, according to their desserts.

7 Gehenna is for the impenitent, other torments for those who can be saved

Some souls, having reached the point of damnation, are rejected from the knowledge of God, and therefore they shall have the pains of Hell without the consolation of deliverance. But some, whom God has not consigned to oblivion, experience a higher process and undergo purgation of the sins into which they have fallen, and at last feel the loosing of their bonds and are delivered into rest. How is this? Gehenna is ready for those who have impenitently forgotten God in their hearts, but other torments for those who, though they perform bad works, do not persevere in them to the end but at last, groaning, look back to God. For this reason let the faithful flee from the Devil and love God, casting away evil works and adorning good works with the beauty of penitence; as My servant Ezekiel, inspired by Me, urges, saying:

8 Words of Ezekiel on this subject

"Be converted, and do penance for all your iniquities; and iniquity shall not be your ruin" [Ez 18:30]. That is to say: O you people! who till now have wallowed in sin, remember your name of Christians, be converted to the way of salvation, and perform all your works in a gush of penitence, who previously had innumerable vices and committed many crimes. Thus as you rise from your evil habits, that iniquity by which you had been soiled will not sink you deep in the ruin of death, since you cast it off in the day of your salvation. Therefore the angels will rejoice over you, because you have abandoned the Devil and run to God, knowing Him better in your good actions than you did when you endured the mockery of the ancient seducer.

9 The Devil's fraud, which deceived Adam through the serpent

That *a loathsome cloud spread out from the pit and touched a deceitful vein-shaped form* means that from the bottom of perdition the Devil's frame came forth and invaded the serpent, who already bore within itself the crime of fraudulent intention, in order to deceive humanity. In what way? Because when the Devil saw

Man in paradise, he cried out with great aversion saying, "Oh! who touches me in the mansion of true beatitude?" And so he knew that he had not yet perfected in any creature the malice he had within himself, but seeing Adam and Eve walk with childlike innocence in the garden of delight, with great wonder he rose up to deceive them through the serpent. Why? Because he understood that the serpent, more than any other animal, resembled him and was eager to accomplish by its deceitfulness what he could not do openly in his own form. So when he saw Adam and Eve run away in soul and body from the forbidden tree, he understood that they were obeying a divine precept, and that in the first work they began he could very easily throw them down.

10 Only from Eve's reply did the Devil know the tree was forbidden

For he would not have known that this tree was forbidden them unless he had proved it by guileful questioning and by their answers. Wherefore *in that bright region he blew upon a white cloud, which had come forth from a beautiful human form and contained within itself many and many stars* because, in that place of delight, Eve—whose soul was innocent, for she had been raised out of innocent Adam, bearing in her body the whole multitude of the human race, shining with God's preordination—was invaded by the Devil through the seduction of the serpent for her own downfall. Why was this? Because he knew that the susceptibility of the woman would be more easily conquered than the strength of the man; and he saw that Adam burned so vehemently in his holy love for Eve that if he, the Devil, conquered Eve, Adam would do whatever she said to him. Hence the Devil *cast out both the cloud and the human form from that region* because that ancient seducer cast out Eve and Adam by his deception from the seat of blessedness and thrust them into the darkness of destruction. How? By first misleading Eve, so that she might flatter and caress Adam and thus win his assent, since she more than any other creature could lead Adam to disobedience, having been made from his rib. Thus woman very quickly overthrows man, if he does not hate her and easily accepts her words.

[Note: Sections 11–25 are not included in this sampler.]

26 After Adam was expelled, God closed Paradise in

But, as you see, after Adam and Eve were expelled from Paradise, *a luminous splendor surrounded that*

30

region, since when they went forth from the place of delight because of their transgression the Power of the Divine Majesty took away every stain of contagion from the place and fortified it with His glory, so that from then on it would be touched by no encroachment; which also showed that the transgression which had taken place there would one day be abolished by His clemency and mercy.

27 Creation opposed Man because he rebelled against God

And so *all the elements of the world, which before had existed in great calm, were turned to the greatest agitation and displayed horrible terrors*, because when Man chose disobedience, rebelling against God and forsaking tranquillity for disquiet, that Creation, which had been created for the service of humanity, turned against humans in great and various ways so that Man, having lowered himself, might be held in check by it. What does this mean? That Man showed himself a rebel against God in the place of delights, and therefore that Creation, which had been subjected to him in service, now opposed itself to him.

31

28 On the delightfulness of Paradise

But Paradise is the place of delight, which blooms with the freshness of flowers and grass and the charms of spices, full of fine odors and dowered with the joy of blessed souls giving invigorating moisture to the dry ground; it supplies strong force to the earth, as the soul gives strength to the body, for Paradise is not darkened by shadow or the perdition of sinners.

29 Why God made Man such that he could sin

Therefore listen and understand me, you who say in your hearts, "What are these things and why?" Oh, why are you so foolish in your hearts, you who have been made in the image and likeness of God? How can such great glory and honor, which is given to you, exist without testing, as if it were an empty case of nothing? Gold must be tested in the fire, and precious stones, to smooth them, must be polished and all things of this kind must be diligently scrutinized. Hence, O foolish humans, how can that which was made in the image and likeness of God exist without testing? For Man must be examined more than any other creature, and therefore he must be tested through every other creature. How?

Spirit is to be tested by spirit, flesh by flesh, earth by

water, fire by cold, fight by resistance, good by evil, beauty by deformity, poverty by riches, sweetness by bitterness, health by sickness, long by short, hard by soft, height by depth, light by darkness, life by death, Paradise by punishments, the Heavenly Kingdom by Gehenna, earthly things by earthly things and heavenly things by heavenly things. Hence Man is tested by every creature, in Paradise, on earth and in Hell: and then he is placed in Heaven. You see clearly only a few things among many that are hidden from your eyes. So why do you deride what is right, plain and just, and good among all good things in the sight of God? Why do you think these things unjust? God is just, but the human race is unjust in transgressing God's precepts when it claims to be wiser than God.

30 Man should not examine the highest things since he cannot the lowest ones

Now tell me, O human: What do you think you were when you were not yet in soul and body? Truly you do not know how you were created. But now, O human, you wish to investigate Heaven and earth, and to judge of their justice in God's disposition, and to know the highest things though you are not able to examine the lowest; for you do not know how you live in the body, or how you may be divested of the body. He Who created you in the first human foresaw all these things; but that same most gentle Father sent His Only-Begotten to die for the people, to deliver humanity from the power of the Devil.

31 *Man now shines brighter in Heaven than before*

And thus Man, having been delivered, shines in God, and God in Man; Man, having community in God, has in Heaven more radiant brightness than he had before. This would not have been so if the Son of God had not put on flesh, for if Man had not remained in Paradise, the Son of God would not have suffered on the cross. But when Man was deceived by the wily serpent, God was touched by true mercy and ordained that His Only-Begotten would become incarnate in the most pure Virgin. And thus after Man's ruin many shining virtues were lifted up in Heaven, like humility, the queen of virtues, which flowered in the virgin birth, and other virtues, which lead God's elect to the heavenly places. For when a field with great labor is cultivated, it brings forth much fruit, and the same is shown in the human race, for after humanity's ruin many virtues arose to raise it up again. But you, O human, oppressed by the heaviness of the flesh, do not see that great glory God's full justice has prepared for you, without stain or unworthiness, so that no one can throw it down. For before the structure of the world was made, God in true justice had foreseen all these things. Therefore, O human, consider this comparison:

32 Man's condition symbolized by a garden, a sheep and a pearl

The master who seeks to set out a garden without being wearied first chooses a suitable site, and then, deciding on a place for each planting, reflects on the fruit of good trees and the utility, taste, fragrance and high esteem of various spices. And so this master, if he is a great philosopher and expert contriver, lays out each of the plantings where he sees that it will be most useful; and then he thinks of enclosing it with great walls, so that none of his enemies can destroy his planting. Then he appoints his experts, who know how to water the garden and who collect its fruit and make from it many fragrant things. Therefore consider well, O human: If that master foresaw that his garden, bringing forth no fruit or any kind of use, was to be destroyed, why would so great a philosopher and contriver have made, planted, watered and fortified it so eagerly and with so much labor?

Hear therefore, and understand! God, Who is the Sun of Justice, made His splendor rise over the filth that is Man's wickedness; and that splendor shone with great brightness, as that filth stank exceedingly. The sun gleamed forth in its brightness, and the filth putrefied in its foulness; and therefore the sun was embraced by those beholding it with much greater love than if the filth had not been there opposite it. Bus as foul as the filth is compared to the sun, so evil is Man's wickedness compared to God's justice. Hence justice, being beautiful, must be loved, and iniquity, being foul, must be rejected.

Into this foulness fell a sheep belonging to the master who had planted this garden. But this sheep was separated from its master by its own consent, not by his negligence; afterward the master sought it again with great zeal and justice. Therefore the choir of angels shone with great honor, for the angels saw a human in Heaven. What does this mean?

When the innocent Lamb was suspended on the cross, the elements trembled, because the most noble

Son of the Virgin was slain in the body by the hands of murderers; by His death the lost sheep was brought back to the pastures of life. For the ancient persecutor saw that because of the blood of the innocent Lamb, which the Lamb had poured out in remission of the sins of humanity, he must lose that sheep, and only then first recognized who that Lamb was; previously he had not been able to understand how the Celestial Bread, without a man's semen and without any desire for sin, had become incarnate of the Virgin by the overshadowing of the Holy Spirit.

For that persecutor, when first he was created, raised himself up in the haughtiness of pride, throwing himself into death and expelling Man from the glory of Paradise; but God did not will to resist him by His power, but conquered him by humility through His Son. And because Lucifer derided God's justice, by God's just judgement he was unable to know the incarnation of God's Only-Begotten. For by this hidden decision the lost sheep was brought back to life. Therefore, O rebellious humans, why are you so hardhearted? God did not will to forsake humanity, but sent His Son for its salvation; thus God crushed the head of pride in the ancient serpent. For when Man was snatched from death, Hell opened its gates, and Satan cried, "Alas, alas, who will help me?" And the Devil's whole band was torn with great agitation, marvelling that there was a power so great they and their prince could not resist it, since they saw the souls of the faithful being taken away from them. Thus Man was lifted up above the heavens because through the Son of God, God appeared in Man and Man in God. Likewise, that master who lost the sheep but brought it so gloriously back to life had, like that sheep, a precious pearl that slipped from him and fell into the mud. But he, not allowing it to lie in the dirt, mercifully drew it forth and purified it of the filth in which it had lain, as gold is purified in the furnace, and restored it to its former honor with even greater glory. For God created Man, but the latter at the Devil's instigation fell into death, from which the Son of God saved him by His blood and brought him gloriously to the glory of Heaven. And how? By humility and charity.

33 Commendation of humility and charity above all other virtues

For humility caused the Son of God to be born of the Virgin, in whom was found humility, not eager embraces or beauty of flesh or earthly riches or gold ornaments or earthly honors. But the Son of God lay in a manger, because His Mother was a poor maiden. Humility always groans, weeps and destroys all offenses, for this is its work. So let anyone who wishes to conquer the Devil arm himself with humility, since Lucifer fervently flees it and hides in its presence like a snake in a hole; for wherever it finds him, it quickly snaps him like a fragile thread.

And charity took the Only-Begotten of God, who was in the bosom of the Father in Heaven, and placed Him in the womb of a mother on earth, for it does not spurn sinners or publicans but seeks to save all. Therefore it often brings forth a fountain of tears from the eyes of the faithful, thus softening hardness of heart. In this, humility and charity are brighter than the other virtues, since humility and charity are like a soul and body that possess stronger powers than the other powers of soul and bodily members. How? Humility is like the soul and charity like the body, and they cannot be separated from each other but work together, just as soul and body cannot be disjoined but work together as long as a person lives in the body. And as the various members of the body are subject, according to their powers, to the soul and to the body, so also the other virtues cooperate, according to their justice, with humility and charity. And therefore, O human, for the glory of God and for your salvation, pursue humility and charity; armed with them, you shall not fear the Devil's snares but shall have everlasting life.

Therefore whoever has knowledge in the Holy Spirit and wings of faith, let this one not ignore My admonition, but taste it, embrace it and receive it in his soul.

FROM BOOK TWO:
THE REDEEMER AND REDEMPTION
VISION ONE
The Redeemer

*A*nd I, a person not glowing with the strength of strong lions or taught by their inspiration, but a tender and fragile rib imbued with a mystical breath, saw a blazing fire, incomprehensible, inextinguishable, wholly living and wholly Life, with a flame in it the color of the sky, which burned ardently with a gentle breath, and which was as inseparably within the blazing fire as the viscera are within a human being. And I saw that the flame sparked and blazed up. And behold! The atmosphere suddenly rose up in a dark sphere of great magnitude, and that flame hovered over it and gave it one blow after another, which struck sparks from it, until that atmosphere was perfected and so Heaven and earth stood fully formed and resplendent. Then the same flame was in that fire, and that burning extended itself to a little clod of mud which lay at the bottom of the atmosphere, and warmed it so that it was made flesh and blood, and blew upon it until it rose up a living human. When this was done, the blazing fire, by means of *that flame which burned ardently with a gentle breath, offered to the human a white flower, which hung in that flame as dew hangs on the grass. Its scent came to the human's nostrils, but he did not taste it with his mouth, or touch it with his hands, and thus he turned away and fell into the thickest darkness, out of which he could not pull himself. And that darkness grew and expanded more and more in the atmosphere. But then three great stars, crowding together in their brilliance, appeared in the darkness, and then many others, both small and large, shining with great splendor, and then a gigantic star, radiant with wonderful brightness, which shot its rays toward the flame. And in the earth too appeared a radiance like the dawn, into which the flame was miraculously absorbed without being separated from the blazing fire. And thus in the radiance of that dawn the Supreme Will was enkindled.*

And as I was trying to ponder this enkindling of the Will more carefully, I was stopped by a secret seal on this vision and I heard the voice from on high saying to me, "You may not see anything further regarding this mystery unless it is granted you by a miracle of faith."

And I saw a serene Man coming forth from this radiant dawn, Who poured out His brightness into the darkness;

and it drove Him back with great force, so that He poured out the redness of blood and the whiteness of pallor into it, and struck the darkness such a strong blow that the person who was lying in it was touched by Him, took on a shining appearance and walked out of it upright. And so the serene Man Who had come out of that dawn shone more brightly than human tongue can tell, and made His way into the greatest height of inestimable glory, where He radiated in the plenitude of wonderful fruitfulness and fragrance. And I heard the voice saying to me from the aforementioned living fire: "O you who are wretched earth and, as a woman, untaught in all learning of earthly teachers and unable to read literature with philosophical understanding, you are nonetheless touched by My light, which kindles in you an inner fire like a burning sun; cry out and relate and write these My mysteries that you see and hear in mystical visions. So do not be timid, but say those things you understand in the Spirit as I speak them through you; so that those who should have shown My people righteousness, but who in their perversity refuse to speak openly of the justice they know, unwilling to abstain from the evil desires that cling to them like their masters and make them fly from the face of tne Lord and blush to speak the truth, may be ashamed. Therefore, O diffident mind, who are taught inwardly by mystical inspiration, though because of Eve's transgression you are trodden on by the masculine sex, speak of that fiery work this sure vision has shown you."

The Living God, then, Who created all things through His Word, by the Word's Incarnation brought back the miserable human, who had sunk himself in darkness, to certain salvation. What does this mean?

1 On God's omnipotence

This blazing fire that you see symbolizes Omnipotent and Living God, Who in His most glorious serenity was never darkened by any iniquity; *incomprehensible*, because He cannot be divided by any division or known as He is by any part of any of His creatures' knowledge; *inextinguishable*, because He is that Fullness that no limit ever touched; *wholly living*, for there is nothing that is hidden from Him or that He does not know; and *wholly Life*, for everything that lives takes its life from Him as Job shows, inspired by Me, when he says:

2 Words of Job on this subject

"Who is ignorant that the hand of the Lord has made all these things? In His hand is the soul of every living thing and the spirit of all human flesh" [Jb 12:9–10]. What does this mean? No creature is so dull of nature as not to know what changes in the things that make it fruitful cause it to attain its full growth. The sky holds light, light air, and air the birds; the earth nourishes plants, plants fruit and fruit animals; which all testify that they were put there by a strong hand, the supreme power of the Ruler of All, Who in His strength has provided so for them all that nothing is lacking to them for their use. And in the omnipotence of the same Maker is the motion of all living things that seek the earth for earthly things like the animals and are not inspired by God with reason, as well as the awakening of those who dwell in human flesh and have reason, discernment and wisdom. How?

The soul goes about in earthly affairs, laboring through many changes as fleshly behavior demands. But the spirit raises itself in two ways: sighing, groaning and desiring God; and choosing among options in various matters as if by some rule, for the soul has discernment in reason. Hence Man contains in himself the likeness of heaven and earth. In what way? He has a circle, which contains his clarity, breath and reason, as the sky has its lights, air and birds; and he has a receptacle containing humidity, germination and birth, as the earth contains fertility, fruition and animals. What is this? O human, you are wholly in every creature and you forget your Creator; you are subject to Him as was ordained, and you go against His commands?

3 That the Word was and is indivisibly and eternally in the Father

You see that *that fire has a flame in the color of the sky, which burns ardently with a gentle breath, and which is as inseparably within the blazing fire as the viscera are within a human being*; which is to say that before any creatures were made the Infinite Word was indivisibly in the Father; Which in course of time was to become incarnate in the ardor of charity, miraculously and without the stain or weight of sin, by the Holy Spirit's sweet freshness in the dawn of blessed virginity. But after He assumed flesh, the Word also remained inseparably in the Father; for as a person does not exist without the vital movements within his viscera, so the only Word of the Father could in no way be separated from Him.

4 Why the Son of God is called the Word

And why is He called the Word? Because, just as a word of command uttered by an instructor among local and transitory human dust is understood by people who know and foresee the reason he gave it, so also the power of the Father is known among the creatures of the world, who perceive and understand in Him the source of their creation, through the Word Who is independent of place and imperishable in His inextinguishable eternal life; and as the power and honor of a human being are known by his official words, so the holiness and goodness of the Father shines through the Supreme Word.

5 *By the power of the Word of God every creature was raised up*

And you see that the *flame sparks and blazes up*. This is to say that when every creature was raised through Him, the Word of God showed His power like a flash of flame; and when He became incarnate in the dawn and purity of virginity, it was as if He blazed up, so that from Him trickled every virtue of the knowledge of God, and Man lived again in the salvation of his soul.

6 *God's incomprehensible power made the world and the different species*

And the atmosphere suddenly rises up in a dark sphere of great magnitude. This is the material of Creation while still formless and imperfect, not yet full of creatures; it is a sphere, for it is under the incomprehensible power of God, which is never absent from it, and by the Supernal Will it rises up in God's great power in the twinkling of an eye. *And that flame hovers over it like a workman and gives it one blow after another, which strike sparks from it, until that atmosphere is perfected and so Heaven and earth stand fully formed and resplendent.* For the Supernal Word, Who excels every creature, showed that they all are subject to Him, and draw their strength from His power, when He brought forth from the universe the different kinds of creatures, shining in their miraculous awakening, as a smith makes forms out of bronze, until each creature was radiant with the loveliness of perfection, beautiful in the fullness of their arrangement in higher and lower ranks, the higher made radiant by the lower and the lower by the higher.

7 After the other creatures Man was created from earthly mud

But then the same flame that is in that fire and that burning extends itself to a little clod of mud, which lies at the bottom of the atmosphere; this is to say that after the other creatures were created, the Word of God, in the strong will of the Father and supernal love, considered the poor fragile matter from which the weak frailty of the human race, both bad and good, was to be produced, now lying in heavy unconsciousness and not yet roused by the breath of life; *and warms it so that it is made flesh and blood*, that is, poured fresh warmth into it, for the earth is the fleshly material of humans, and nourished it with moisture, as a mother gives milk to her children; *and blows upon it until it rises up a living human*, for He aroused it by supernal power and miraculously raised up a human being with intelligence of body and mind.

8 Adam accepted obedience, but by the Devil's counsel did not obey

When this is done, the blazing fire, by means of that flame which burns ardently with a gentle breath, offers to the human a white flower, which hangs in that flame as dew hangs on the grass. For, after Adam was created, the Father in His lucid serenity gave to Adam through His Word in the Holy Spirit the sweet precept of obedience, which in fresh fruitfulness hung upon the Word; for the sweet odor of sanctity trickled from the Father in the Holy Spirit through the Word and brought forth fruit in greatest abundance, as the dew falling on the grass makes it grow. *Its scent comes to the human's nostrils, but he does not taste it with his mouth or touch it with his hands*; for he tried to know the wisdom of the Law with his intelligence, as if with his nose, but did not perfectly digest it by putting it in his mouth, or fulfill it in full blessedness by the work of his hands. *And thus he turns away and falls into the thickest darkness, out of which he cannot pull himself.* For, by the Devil's counsel, he turned his back on the divine command and sank into the gaping mouth of death, so that he did not seek God either by faith or by works; and therefore, weighed down by sin, he could not rise to true knowledge of God, until He came Who obeyed His Father sinlessly and fully.

And that darkness grows and expands more and more in the atmosphere; for the power of death in the world was constantly increased by the spread of wickedness, and human knowledge entangled itself in many vices in the horror of bursting and sinking sin.

9 Abraham and Isaac and Jacob and the other prophets drove back the darkness

But then three great stars, crowding together in their brilliance, appear in the darkness, and then many others, both small and large, shining with great splendor. These are the three great luminaries Abraham, Isaac and Jacob, symbolizing the Heavenly Trinity, embracing one another both by their works of faith and by their relationship in the flesh, and by their signs driving back the darkness in the world; and, following them, the many other prophets both minor and major, radiant with many wonders.

10 The prophet John, glittering with miracles, foretold the Son of God

And then a gigantic star appears, radiant with wonderful brightness, which shoots its rays toward the flame. This is the greatest prophet, John the Baptist, who glittered with miracles in his faithful and serene deeds, and pointed out by their means the true Word, the true Son of God; for he did not yield to wickedness, but vigorously and forcefully cast it out by works of justice.

11 At the Incarnation of the Word of God the great counsel was seen

And in the earth too appears a radiance like the dawn, into which the flame is miraculously absorbed, without being separated from the blazing fire. This is to say that

God set a great splendor of light in the place where He would bring forth His Word and, fully willing it, sent Him there, yet not so as to be divided from Him; but He gave that profitable fruit and brought Him forth in a great fountain, so that every faithful throat could drink and never more be dry. *And thus in the radiance of that dawn the Supreme Will is enkindled*; for in the bright and roseate serenity was seen the fruitfulness of the great and venerable counsel, so that all the fore-runners marvelled at it with bright joy.

12 Humans must not scrutinize God's secrets beyond what He wishes to show

But you, O human, who seek in the way of humans to know more fully the loftiness of this counsel, are opposed by a concealing barrier; for you must not search into the secrets of God beyond those things the Divine Majesty wills to be revealed for love of those who trust in Him.

13 Christ by His death brought back His elect to their inheritance

And you see a serene Man coming forth from this radi-ant dawn. Who pours out His brightness into the dark-

ness; and it drives Him back with great force, so that He pours out the redness of blood and the whiteness of pallor into it, and strikes the darkness such a strong blow that the person who is lying in it is touched by Him, takes on a shining appearance and walks out of it upright. This is the Word of God, imperishably incarnate in the purity of unstained virginity and born without pain, and yet not separated from the Father. How? While the Son of God was being born in the world from a mother, He was still in Heaven in the Father; and at this the angels suddenly trembled and sang the sweetest praises of rejoicing. And, living in the world without stain of sin, He sent out into the darkness of unbelief His clear and blessed teachings and salvation; but, rejected by the unbelieving people and led to His Passion, He poured out His beautiful blood and knew in His body the darkness of death. And thus conquering the Devil, He delivered from Hell His elect, who were held prostrate there, and by His redeeming touch brought them back to the inheritance they had lost in Adam. As they were returning to their inheritance timbrels and harps and all kinds of music burst forth, because Man, who had lain in perdition but now stood upright in blessedness, had been freed by heavenly power and escaped from death, as through My servant Hosea I have stated thus:

14 *Words of Hosea on this subject*

"The iniquity of Ephraim is bound up; his sin is hidden. The sorrows of a woman in labor shall come upon him; he is an unwise son; for now he shall not stand in the contrition of the sons. I will deliver them out of the hand of death, from death I will redeem them. I will be your death, O Death; I will be your destruction, O Hell!" [Hos 13:12–14]. What does this mean? The Devil's perverse iniquity is bound by heavy fetters, since he does not deserve that God's zeal should release him; for he has never rightfully acknowledged Him as do those who faithfully fear Him. For the Devil always raises himself against God, saying, "I am God!"; and he always goes astray over the Blessed One of the Lord, opposing the name of Christians because of Him. Thus his malice is so ingrained that his sin, cruelly committed in filthy pride, can never deserve by any reparation to be covered by salvation. Therefore he will be in perpetual pain, as a woman in labor is afflicted by despair when she doubts she can survive the opening of her womb. For this misery will remain with him, that he is forsaken by beatitude because the wisdom of the sons flees from him, and he does not come to himself, as that man came to himself who returned to his father from his wickedness.

Thus he will never stand trusting in that action by which the children of salvation in the Heavenly Son crush death in its hardened iniquity, which the cunning serpent brought forth when he suggested deceit to the guileless first man. But since those children despise the poison of that unclean advice and look to their salvation, I will deliver them from slavery to idols; for idols are by their deceptiveness in the power of perdition, and for them the unfaithful forsake the honor of their Creator, entangling themselves in the Devil's snare and doing his works at his will.

And so I will redeem the souls of those who love and worship Me, the Holy and the Just, from the pain of Hell; for no one can be released from the Devil's fetters, which bind him with bitterest death by his transgression of God's precepts, except by the redemption of Him Who will redeem His elect with His own blood. This is how I will slay you, O Death, with utter destruction, for I will take from you the thing you think to live by, and you will be called a useless corpse; at the height of your strength you will lie prostrate, as a corpse without the soul lies prostrate awaiting decay. For when the happy souls are mercifully raised up to celestial bliss through the new Man, Who will not be a party to poisonous deception, the fountain of living water will drown you. Thus also to your confusion I will be your destruction, O Hell!, when my strong power will take from you your ill-gotten spoils, so that you too, justly despoiled, will never again appear whole and laden with riches, but will lie prostrate and confounded forever, bearing wounds and decay.

15 The Son of God rising from the dead showed Man the way from death to life

And, as you see, *the serene Man Who has come out of that dawn shines more brightly than human tongue can tell*, which shows that the noble body of the Son of God, born of the sweet Virgin and three days in the tomb (to confirm that there are three Persons in one Divinity), was touched by the glory of the Father, received the Spirit and rose again to serene immortality, which no one can explain by thought or word. And the Father showed Him with His open wounds to the celestial choirs, saying, "This is My beloved Son, Whom I sent to die for the people." And so joy unmeasurable by the

human mind arose in them, for criminal forgetfulness
of God was brought low, and human reason, which had
lain prostrate under the Devil's persuasion, was uplifted
to the knowledge of God; for the way to truth was
shown to Man by the Supreme Beatitude, and in it he
was led from death to life.

6 The risen Christ appeared frequently to His disciples

But just as the children of Israel, after being liberated
from Egypt, wandered in the desert for forty years
before coming into the land flowing with milk and
honey, so too the Son of God, rising from the dead,
showed Himself for forty days to His disciples and the
blessed women who wept and had a great desire to see
Him. This He did to encourage them, lest they should
waver in faith and say, "We did not see Him, so we cannot believe that He is our salvation!" He showed
Himself to them frequently, to strengthen them that
they might not fall.

7 When Christ ascended to the Father His Bride was given many ornaments

*And He makes His way into the greatest height of ines-
timable glory, where he radiates in the plenitude of wonder-*

ful fruitfulness and fragrance. This is to say that the So
of God ascended to the Father, Who with the Son an
the Holy Spirit is the height of lofty and excelling jo
and gladness unspeakable; where that same Son glor
ously appears to His faithful in the abundance of san
tity and blessedness, so that they believe with pure an
simple hearts that He is true God and Man. And the
indeed the new Bride of the Lamb was set up with man
ornaments, for she had to be ornamented with ever
kind of virtue for the mighty struggle of all the faithf
people, who are to fight against the crafty serpent.

But let the one who sees with watchful eyes an
hears with attentive ears welcome with a kiss My my
tical words, which proceed from Me Who am life.

God and Man

A nd I, a person taken up from among other people—
though unworthy to be called a human, since I
ve transgressed God's law and have been unjust
en I should have been just, except that by God's
ace I am His creature and will be saved—I looked
ward the East. And there *I saw a single block of stone,
measurably broad and high and the color of iron, with
white cloud above it; and above the cloud a royal throne,
und in shape, on which One was sitting, living and shin-
g and marvelous in His glory, and so bright that I could
t behold Him clearly. He held to His breast what looked
e black and filthy mire, as big as a human heart, sur-
unded with precious stones and pearls.*

*And from this Shining One seated upon the throne
tended a great circle colored gold like the dawn, whose
dth I could not take in; it circled about from the East to
e North and to the West and to the South, and back*

59

toward the East to the Shining One, and had no end. A
that circle was so high above the earth that I could r
apprehend it; and it shone with a terrifying radiance
color of stone, steel and fire, which extended everywhe
from the heights of Heaven to the depth of the abyss,
that I could see no end to it.

And then I saw a great star, splendid and beautif
come forth from the One seated on the throne. And w
that star came a great multitude of shining sparks, wh
followed the star toward the South, looking on the O
seated on the throne like a stranger; they turned away fr
Him and stared toward the North instead of contemplat
Him. But, in the very act of turning away their gaze, t
were all extinguished and were changed into black cinde

And behold, a whirlwind arose from those cinde
which drove them away from the South, behind the O
sitting on the throne, and carried them to the Nor
where they were precipitated into the abyss and vanish
from my sight. But when they were extinguished, I s
the light, which was taken from them, immediat
return to Him Who sat on the throne.

And I heard the One Who sat on the throne sayi
to me, "Write what you see and hear." And, from t
inner knowledge of that vision, I replied, "I besee

you, my Lord, give me understanding, that by my account I may be able to make known these mystical things; forsake me not, but strengthen me by the daylight of Your justice, in which Your Son was manifested. Grant me to make known the divine counsel, which was ordained of old, as I can and should: how You willed Your Son to become incarnate and become a human being within Time; which You willed before all creation in Your rectitude and the fire of the Dove, the Holy Spirit, so that Your Son might rise from a Virgin in the splendid beauty of the sun and be clothed with true humanity, a man's form assumed for Man's sake."

And I heard Him say to me, "Oh, how beautiful are your eyes, which tell of divinity when the divine counsel dawns in them!" And again I answered from the inner knowledge of the vision, "To my own inner soul I seem as filthy ashes of ashes and transitory dust, trembling like a feather in the dark. But do not blot me out from the land of the living, for I labor at this vision with great toil. When I think of the worthlessness of my foolish bodily senses, I deem myself the least and lowest of creatures; I am not worthy to be called a human being, for I am exceedingly afraid and do not dare to recount Your mysteries. O good and kind Father, teach me what to say according to Your will! O reverend Father, sweet and full of grace, do not forsake me, but keep me in Your mercy!"

And again I heard the same One saying to me, "Now speak, as you have been taught! Though you are ashes, I will that you speak. Speak of the revelation of the bread, which is the Son of God, Who is life in the fire of love; Who raises up everyone dead in soul and body, forgives all repented sins in His serene clarity, and awakens holiness in a person and sets it growing. Thus God, the magnificent, glorious and incomprehensible, gave Him as a great intercessor by sending Him into the purity of the Virgin, who had no corruptible weakness in her virginity. No pollution of the flesh should or could have been in the mind of the Virgin; for when the Son of God came in silence into the dawn, which was the humble maiden, Death, the slayer and destroyer of the human race, was deceived without knowing it as if in a dream. Death went on securely, not realizing what life that sweet Virgin bore, for her virginity had been hidden from it. And that Virgin was poor in worldly goods, for the Divine Majesty willed to have her so. Now write about the true knowledge of the Creator in His goodness."

1 The faithful should venerate the magnitude of the fear of the Lord

God, Who created all things and appointed humanity to that glory from which the lost angel and his followers were cast out, should be worshipped and feared by every creature of His with the greatest honor and awe; for it is just that His creatures should worship the Creator of all things and faithfully adore God above all beings. This is symbolized by that stone that you see. For in this mystery it represents the magnitude of the fear of God, which should always arise and live in the hearts of the faithful with purest purpose.

You see it as *a single block of stone, immeasurably broad and high and the color of iron*; this shows how firmly the fear of God must be held. For God is to be dreaded by every creature with single-heartedness, so that they know He is the one true God, without Whom is no one and like Whom there is no one. *It has immense breadth*, because He is incomprehensible; *and height*, because Divinity is above all else and the highest pitch of any creature's senses cannot understand or attain to it. *Its iron color* means that it is burdensome and hard for human minds to fear God; for this is a heavy burden for soft and fragile dust, and the human creature rebels against it.

2 *Every soul that wisely fears God becomes by faith God's throne*

The white cloud above that stone is the clear wisdom of the human mind; and *the royal throne above the cloud, round in shape*, is the strong faith of the Christian people. In it, God is faithfully recognized; for wherever the fear of the Lord takes root, human wisdom will also appear, and then God's help will set faith above it, and prepare His rest in it. For when God is feared, He is understood by faith with the help of human wisdom, and these will touch Him as a seat touches its owner. And in them God prepares a seat for Himself, supreme above all else; for neither power nor force can comprehend Him, but He resides in single-minded and pure faith, One above all things.

3 *God's mystery is incomprehensible unless He gives faith to do so*

And One is sitting on that throne, living and shining and marvelous in His glory, and so bright that you cannot behold Him clearly. He holds to His breast what looks like

*black and filthy mire, as big as a human heart, surrounded
with precious stones and pearls.* This is the Living God,
Who reigns over all things, shining in goodness and
wondrous in His works. The deep mystery of His
immense glory can never be perfectly contemplated by
anyone, unless faith allows that person to comprehend
and bear Him, as a seat contains and surrounds its
owner. As the seat is subject to its owner and cannot rise
and throw him off, so faith has no proud desire to look
upon God, but only touches Him in intimate devotion.

4 In the Father's wisdom the perfection of the elect is revealed

And to His breast, that is in the wisdom of His mystery, for love of His Son He holds that poor, weak,
infirm mire that is Man: black in the blackness of sins
and filthy in the filthiness of the flesh, but the size of a
human heart, which is the breadth of the profound wisdom with which God created Man. For He has looked
upon those who are saving their souls through penitence, and no matter how in their persistent weakness
they have sinned against Him, they will come to Him at
last. They are surrounded by ornaments, those great
ones who rise up among them: martyrs and holy virgins

like precious stones, and innocent and penitent children of redemption like pearls; so that by them the mire is surpassingly adorned, and the virtues, which so gloriously shine in God, shine also in the human body. For He Who put breath and life in Man was scrutinizing Himself. How?

Because He foreknew and decided in advance that His Son would be incarnate to bring redemption; therefore, every stain of sin must be washed away from His body. And so too He knows the souls which, after many and great sins while they are still in the body, will end by being justified; which, after their several errors will walk in God's justice, will be steadfast in Him and shake off their forgetfulness, turning from the vices that wounded them in the earthly places where they fell into sin. And He will also take note of the fact that many peoples have arisen from their erring ways and were brought back from the deadly stench of sin, though they were walking covered with wounds and most dreadful sores; but many will arise who have been wounded so severely by the bitter and harsh pains of sin that their crimes are beyond measure and their evil habits are ingrained, and they are too ill even to summon the energy to do their deadly works, murder and adultery and all the other evils.

5 Example from the Gospel

O wretches! Do they not approach like pilgrims from a far-off land? As the Scripture says in the Gospel, the younger son said, "I will arise and go to my father and say to him, 'Father, I have sinned against Heaven and before you, and am no longer worthy to be called your son. Make me as one of your hired servants'" [Lk 15:18]. This is to say: A person who, admonished by the Holy Spirit, comes to himself after a fall into sin says, "I want to rise up from the unendurable sins whose heavy guilt I can no longer bear. I will retrace my steps in memory, lamenting and sorrowing over my sins, until I come to my Father, Who is my Father because He created me. And I will say to him, 'Father, I have sinned against Heaven, wronging the celestial work that is myself; You formed me by Your will, and touched me in creating me, so that I should be only celestial in my deeds, but I have belittled myself by shameful actions. And I have sinned before You, because I have forsaken the humanity of my nature. How? By my many abominations.

" 'Therefore, I am guilty both of losing myself and insulting You, and am not worthy to be called Your Son; for in the wickedness of my heart I have led Your creature in me in a path You did not appoint for me. But now, let me be as Your servant, redeemed at the price of Your Son's blood. You gave Him at a price so great that not even death can ever repay it; but that price allows penitence to arise from Your Son's Passion, and so sets sinners free. I have lost my rightful inheritance as a child of Adam, for he, who was created a son in justice, was stripped of that joyful glory; but now the blood of Your Son and penitence have redeemed the sins of humanity.' "

And thus all should speak who have repeated Adam's fall but then return through penitence and attain to salvation. They should remember the many warnings they have heard told from the Scriptures about the suffering and the blood of their Redeemer, and recall with lamentation how they have transgressed the rules of keeping God's word instead of receiving them with longing. For they neglected His law, which was set up for them to keep when the commandments were instituted, and refused to think about what things they should have done and left undone for fear of the Lord. But they come to the truth nonetheless, remembering what they heard and learned from God; even though they previously were blinded, not desiring to know His justice and avoiding whatever would set that justice they despised above their sins; even though they turned their backs on God's word and rejected His law.

Many of these will be superabundant in good things; they will not find it sufficient to feast in the house of the Lord, to celebrate His Divine Office and work His justice to the fullest, but will always be weeping and woefully remembering the evils they did when they cherished unlawful works and ignored the deeds God's law allowed.

6 *The meaning of the mire on the breast and why the angels may not spurn Man*

This is the filthy mire that you see on the breast of the loving Father. How? The Son of God went forth from the Father's heart and entered into the world; He is surrounded by the people who believe, and by their decision so believe in Him, hold to Him. And therefore they also appear on the breast of the gentle Father; and thus neither angel nor any other creature may spurn a human being, since the incarnate Son of the Most High

God has human form in Himself. For the blessed choir of angels would regard Man as unworthy, for he stinks of vice and sin, while those heavenly angels themselves are invulnerable and free from any deed of injustice; except that they continually see the face of the Father, and love in the Son what is loved by the Father. What is this? That the Son of God was born as a human. For I, the Father, established My Son, born of the Virgin, for the salvation and restoration of humanity, as My servant, the prophet Isaiah, says to you:

7 Words of Isaiah

"He shall feed His flock like a shepherd. He shall gather up the lambs with His arm and raise them to His bosom; and He shall carry those who are with young"[Is 40:11]. Which is to say: As a shepherd feeds his flock, so My Son, the Good Shepherd, feeds the flock of His redeemed. How? He feeds it by His law, which He planted through Me. Because My Son is human, He will extend His power like His arm, and gather together the lambs, who by the innocence of baptism, which strips from them the old man and his works, are innocent of Adam's sin; and by His virtues and His law He will take them up into His bosom. How? By lifting them above the height of the heavens and making them members of Himself.

Therefore the human form is to be seen in the inmost nature of the Deity, where neither angels nor any other creatures appear; because My Only-Begotten, to redeem the human race assumed human form in the flesh of a Virgin. And He will carry in His heart those who are with young. How? My Son carries human beings in His blood, and saves them by His five wounds, for whatever sins they have committed by means of their five senses are washed away by supreme justice when they repent; and He carries them so because He was incarnate, and suffered wounds on the cross, and died and was buried, and rose again from the dead.

And He has stretched out His hand to them and drawn them back to Himself. How? When He assumed humanity for them, though they thought they were lost when Adam fell. For My Only-Begotten conquered death, and it could no longer triumph over them; and so He knew them in the power of His glory, and knew that they were to come to Him by the purgation of penance.

And you see them appear in the bosom of the

Father. This means that the Son of Man is perfected with all His members in the secret heart of His Father. How? Because when the world reaches its end, the elect of Christ, who are His members, are to be perfected. O how beautiful is He! As the Psalmist says:

8 Words of David

"Beautiful of form above the children of men" [Ps 44:3]. This is to say: In Him shines forth beauty beyond beauty, the noblest form free from any spot of sin, without a splash of human corruption, and lacking all desire for the sinful works demanded by fleshly human weakness. None of these ever touched this Man. And the body of the Son of Man was born more purely than other people, for the stainless Virgin bore her Son in ignorance of sin, and thus ignorant of the sorrow of childbirth. How? She never felt any stubborn urge to sin, and therefore the pains of childbirth were unknown to her; but the wholeness of her body rejoiced within her. Oh, how beautiful then His body!

But let the people know that His bodily beauty was no greater than the profound wisdom that established His human form; for the Father, the Son and the Holy Spirit, one God in Three Persons, does not delight in the beauty of the flesh but in the humility with which the Son of God clothed Himself in humanity. And in His form there were no exterior blemishes. Sometimes an ordinary person is given by God an ugly appearance as bodies go, as when his limbs are distorted and misshapen and he is a cripple. This is not because nature forms human bodies, but because of God's judgment; a strong nature is expressed in a proper form, and a weak one in various deformities. But the latter was not the case with My Son.

Humans, I say, are widely divergent in bodily form; they can be black, ugly, polluted, leprous, dropsical and full of defects; they can also be persuaded by devilish art into becoming inflamed with sorcery, stupid, blind to the good things of the Lord or forgetful of what they should praise and what they should blame. For they should do the works of justice, but they do the works of evil and omit the good, despising the cross and the martyrdom of their Lord. But God the Father contemplates this work of mire with the purpose of His goodness, as a father looks at his children when he hugs them to his breast. And, because He is God, He has the love of a tender father for his children. For so great is His heart's inmost love for people that He sent His Son to the cross, like a meek lamb that is carried to the slaughter. And so the Son brought back the lost sheep, bearing them on His shoulder by assuming humanity; which caused Him great sufferings, for He deigned to die for His flock.

But among these people there are many surrounded by ornaments and adorned pricelessly with virtue. They are the martyrs, the virgins, the innocents and the penitents, as I said before, and those who have obeyed their masters, and those who accuse themselves of their sins and tirelessly strive to punish themselves for them, denying the self in them. And who or where these elect are must not be stated; for the numbers of them all have been reckoned.

Does anyone think it possible to see into the deep wisdom of the Most High and into the discernment of His knowledge, and count the number of those who are to be saved? His judgments are incomprehensible to all people. Your task is to run; for the kingdom of God is prepared for you. For as great as is the zeal of the faithful, washed in baptism and known in faith, to fulfil God's justice, so great also shall be their reward.

9 The Father does, ordains and perfects all His works through His Son

But you see that *from the One seated upon the throne extends a great circle colored gold like the dawn, whose width you cannot take in*. This means that from the Almighty Father there extends a supremely strong power and action, whose might encircles all things; and He works it through His Son, Who is always with Him in the majesty of Divinity, ordaining and perfecting all His works through Him before all worlds and in the world from its start. His Son glows with the brilliant beauty of the dawn; for He was incarnate in the wisest Virgin, whom the dawn signifies, by the hand of God Which is the Holy Spirit, in Whom also each work of the Father is done. You can never comprehend the full extent of His glory, for no creature has, will have, or should have a standard of goodness or power with which to measure His power or His deeds; God's power is inestimable and incomprehensible, and His works are invincible and marvelous.

10 On the revolving circle

And that circle wheels about from the East to the North and to the West and to the South, and back toward the

East to the One on the throne, and has no end. This is to say that God's power and His work encircle and include every creature. How? All creatures arose in the will of the Father, Who is One God with the Son and the Holy Spirit, and all feel Him in His power. How? They all feel Him in their creation: He wheels around from the East, the origin of all justice, to the North, where the Devil is confounded, to the West, where the darkness of death tries to extinguish the light of life but the light conquers it and rises again, and to the South, where the ardor of God's justice burns in the hearts of the faithful; and so back to the rising of justice as to the East. What does this mean?

When in God's foreordained time His work shall have been completed in the people of this world, then the circuit of the world will have been made, and the perfection of time and the last day will arrive; and then each work of God, seated in His throne without end, will shine resplendent in His elect. For God is perfect in His power and His work, Who was and is and ever shall be, and His Divinity had no beginning; so that it is not that He will have been, but that He is.

11 God's power is greater than Man can know, and why the angels praise Him

And that circle is so high above the earth that you cannot apprehend it. This is to say that the Supreme Power is so far exalted above the lives of all creatures and above the sense and intellect of Man, and so incomprehensible in and above all, that no creature's senses can grasp it, except to realize that this Power is much higher than it can know. And therefore the angels sing to God in praise; for they see Him in His power and glory, but they also cannot understand or sense Him completely, and they can never have enough of His magnitude or His beauty.

12 God is manifest justice, true and just without alteration

But that *it shines with a terrifying radiance the color of stone, steel and fire*; this means that the divine power radiates formidable and severe virtue against iniquity that is dissimulated, impenitent or unpunished. This strength is like steel, because God's manifest justice yields nothing to weak injustice; whereas dust, as the saying goes, is unjust and does not please God. His justice, like steel, strengthens all other justice, which is weaker than it, as iron is weaker than steel. And this strength is like fire; for He Himself is the Fire of Judgment, burning up all sin and injustice, which refused to bow down before Him and seek His mercy.

And God is like the rock in Man; for He is true and just without any alteration, as stone cannot be changed into softness. He is like steel, piercing everything with His all-penetrating gaze, never changing but remaining God of all things. And He is also like fire, because He inflames and enkindles and illuminates all things without changing over time; for He is God.

13 God's strength, justice and judgment have no boundary Man can sense

And you see that *this radiance extends everywhere, from the heights of Heaven to the depth of the abyss, so that you can see no end to it.* This is to say that the strength of God's power and work, His justice and His upright judgment are everywhere, and neither in the heights of Heaven nor in the depths of the abyss is there any boundary to them that human senses can comprehend.

14 Why and how the first angel and his followers fell

Then you see a great star, splendid and beautiful, come forth from the One seated on the throne, and with that star come a great multitude of shining sparks. For, by the command of the Almighty Father, the angel Lucifer, who now is Satan, came forth from his beginnings adorned with great glory and clothed with brightness and beauty; and with him came all the lesser lights that were his followers, who then shone with brightness but now are extinguished in darkness. But he was inclined toward evil and did not look on Me the Perfect One; he trusted in himself and thought he could begin anything he wished and finish anything he began. Thus the great honor he owed to the One on the throne, Who was his creator, he gave to himself, and so descended into sin.

But all the sparks that follow the star toward the South look on the One seated on the throne like a stranger; they turn away from Him and stare toward the North instead of contemplating Him. This is to say that Lucifer and all his company, who were miraculously created by the ardent goodness of God, had a secret sin, which was that their pride disdained the One Who reigns in Heaven. All of them, formed at the beginning of Creation , tasted the impiety that leads to perdition, and contemplated God not in order to know His goodness but in order to exalt themselves above Him as if He were a stranger; in their open elation they turned away from knowledge of Him in His glory and hastened toward their fall. *But, in the very act of turning away their gaze, they are all extinguished and are changed into black cinders.* Which is to say that as soon as they disdained to know God, the splendid brilliance with which the divine power had clothed them was extinguished in Lucifer himself and all the followers of his malice; as he destroyed in himself the inner beauty that was his consciousness of good, and gave himself over to impiety, he was erased from eternal glory and fell into eternal loss. Therefore they were all changed into black cinders; stripped of their bright splendor along with their leader, the Devil, they were smothered in darkness and deprived of the glory of beatitude, like a dead coal without its smoldering spark.

Then a whirlwind arises from those cinders, which drives them away from the South, behind the One sitting on the throne, and carries them to the North, where they are precipitated into the abyss and vanish from your sight. This is to say that when these angels of iniquity tried to prevail over God and oppress Him with their pride, the wind of impiety that arose in them was belched forth in bitter perdition, and blew them backward from the

South, which means from goodness, into the North, which means into forgetfulness of God the Ruler of all. Thus when they tried to exalt themselves in pride, they were confounded and met their downfall, and were precipitated by their pride into the abyss of eternal death, which is their doom, never again to be seen in brightness. Even so did I tell the noonday forest, which should ardently have borne the fruit of justice and did not, by My servant Ezekiel:

15 Words of Ezekiel

"Behold, I will kindle a fire in you and will burn in you every green tree and every dry tree. The flame of the fire shall not be quenched; and every face shall be burned in it, from the south to the north. And all flesh shall see that it is I the Lord Who have kindled it; and it shall not be quenched" [Ez 20:47–48]. Which is to say: O fool, who raised yourself up in pride against Me! I Who have neither beginning nor end will bring this to pass: In My zeal I will kindle in you the fire of My wrath, and burn up all your vigor with which you tried to begin a work, trusting in your false energy more than in Me, and choosing to act as your pride dictated on your own foolish wisdom. And I will burn up in you all your dryness, that aridity which belongs to your sin and that of the other lost ones, and in which you tempt humanity, which is ashes, to sin; and this temptation will not bring you back salvation, but will become in you eternal fire. There is no reward of salvation for you or those who follow your example. And that fire of punishment shall not be quenched or abate its tortures, but will burn up that headlong pride in which you looked upon the face of honor and tried to seize it for yourself. And thus were you ejected from all your glory; you rose in the South in clear and ardent light, but you set in the darkness of the North, which is to say in Hell.

And everyone shall see this and know Gehenna, both the elect and the reprobate. The elect will know Gehenna because they have escaped it, and the reprobate because they will remain in it and be punished; knowing that it is the place that I the Lord Almighty have kindled in retribution for your crimes, O Devil, and it will not be extinguished by your evil deeds or those of your followers. So the sin of diabolical pride has cast Satan and his angels into the outer darkness of eternal torment, without any comfort from light; so that there is no place for them in the eternal light, and you, O frail human, cannot see them there any longer. As Ezekiel, imbued with My Spirit, says with mystical significance to the king of Tyre:

"All who see you among the nations will be astonished at you; you are brought to naught, and you shall not be forevermore" [Ez 28:19]. Which is to say: All the upright of heart, O Devil, will be astounded at your filthiness, seeing you drunken with the vices of the nations who embrace you and transgress the laws of God and wither away; for you pollute with temptation God's temple, which is Man. And so, through your pride you are brought to naught and fall from the glory of salvation; for you have no honor and no felicity, and no glory shall be yours in the eternity of Heaven; you are lost from them forever, without end.

16 The glory lost by the Devil and the others was saved by the Father

But when they are extinguished, you see the light that was taken from them immediately return to Him Who sits on the throne. This is to say that when the Devil, because of his pride and obstinacy, lost his exceeding brilliance, (for Lucifer was of purer light than all the other angels), and when the seeds of death entered into him and all his followers, that brilliance returned to God the Father to be kept in His secret heart; for the glory of that splendor was not allowed to go for nothing, but God kept it as a light for another of His creations.

For God, Who commanded one variety of His creatures to arise without flesh yet bright in splendor, namely the Devil and all his company, kept this splendor for the mire that He formed into Man, who arose covered with a vile earthly nature, that he might not exalt himself into the likeness of God. For the one created in bright splendor, and not clothed in a miserable form as humans are, could not sustain his self-exaltation; there is only one Eternal God, without beginning or end. And thus comparing oneself to God is the wickedest of all crimes.

And so I, the God of Heaven, kept the illustrious light, which departed from the Devil because of his crime, and hid it within Myself until I gave it to the mire of the earth, which I had formed in My image and likeness; as does a human being when his son dies and his inheritance cannot pass to children of his. When he has no children to inherit, a father holds the inheritance and plans to give it to children yet unborn, and when they are born from him he gives it to them.

17 *The Devil fell without leaving an heir, but fallen Man had one*

For the Devil fell without leaving an heir, which is to say without the intention of doing good works; he never accomplished or began anything good, and therefore another received his inheritance. This other also fell, but did have an heir, which was the beginning of obedience; and he received this inheritance with devotion, even though he could not complete the work that went with it. But then God's grace completed that work in the Incarnation of the Savior of the nations, and restored the good inheritance. So Man receives his inheritance in Christ, because he did not reject God's commandments when they were first given; whereas the Devil did not want to serve the Creator for good, but to vaunt his own pride, and so was deprived of the glory and perished in perdition.

18 *Example of Goliath and David*

As Goliath rose up despising David, so the Devil rose up presuming upon himself and wanting to be like the

Most High. And as Goliath was unaware of David's strength and despised him as nothing, so the Devil's towering pride despised the humility of the Son of God's humanity, when He was born into the world and sought not His own glory but in all things the glory of the Father. How? The Devil did not seek to imitate this example and submit himself to his Creator as the Son of God submitted Himself to His Father. But David, with the secret strength given to him by God, cut off Goliath's head, as is written by the inspiration of the Holy Spirit:

"And David, taking the head of the Philistine, carried it into Jerusalem; but his arms he placed in his own tent" [1 Kgs 17:54]. This is to say: My Son took the spoils and booty of the Devil with His great power and deprived the ancient serpent of his head. Where? In the womb of the Virgin, who crushed that head. Through whom? Through her Son. What is this crushing? The holy humility, which appears both in the Mother and in the Son, and struck at the origin of pride, which is the head of the Devil. And so, in His humility My Son in the body carried that head into the holy Church, which is the vision of peace, and showed it that the pride of the Devil had been slain.

The strong arms are the Devil's stubborn vices, by which he had overcome the human race and made them worship him as God; for he had terrified them by his vices as people are terrified by arms. But My Son broke them and placed them in His tent; that is, in the Passion of His body while He suffered on the cross.

So now He lets the battle continue among the tents, which are the bodies of His chosen members, that they may divide with Him the Devil's arms. How? As He conquered the Devil in His Passion, they too may conquer him by restraining themselves from their desires and not being in harmony with his vices. And, to extend the metaphor, as the glory of Goliath was given to David, so the glory that was taken from the first angel was given by Me to Adam and his race, which confesses Me and keeps My precepts, after the Devil's pride was destroyed.

But let the one who has ears sharp to hear inner meanings ardently love My reflection and pant after My words, and inscribe them in his soul and conscience.

SUGGESTIONS FOR FURTHER READING

Hildegard of Bingen: Scivias. Translated by Mother Columba Hart and Jane Bishop. Classics of Western Spirituality Series. Paulist Press, 1990.

Hildegard of Bingen: Mystic, Healer, Companion of Angels. Ingeborg Ulrich. Liturgical Press, 1993.

Hildegard of Bingen: Mystical Writings. Edited by Fiona Bowie. Spiritual Classics Series. Crossroad Publishing Company, 1990.

Hildegard of Bingen: The Book of the Rewards of Life (Liber Vitae Meritorum). Translated by Bruce W. Hozeski. Library of Medieval Literature, vol. 89b. Garland, 1993.

Hildegard of Bingen (1098–1179): A Visionary Life. Sabina Flanagan. Routledge, 1989.

Hildegard of Bingen's Book of Divine Works with Letters and Songs. Edited by Matthew C. Fox. Bear & Co., 1987.

Hildegard of Bingen's Medicine. Wighard Strehlow and Gottfried Hertzka. Folk Wisdom Series. Bear & Co., 1987.

The Letters of Hildegard of Bingen, vol. 1. Translated by Joseph L. Baird and Radd K. Ehrmann. Oxford University Press, 1994.

OTHER BOOKS IN THE SERIES

TRUE JOY:
THE WISDOM OF FRANCIS AND CLARE

THE LIFE OF THE SOUL:
THE WISDOM OF JULIAN OF NORWICH

EVERYTHING AS DIVINE:
THE WISDOM OF MEISTER ECKHART